THE
Empowered
PARENT

THE
Empowered
PARENT

KRISTEN MAKRUSH

www.ahigherlife.com

The Empowered Parent: Navigating the Special Needs Diagnosis of Your Child by Kristen Makrush

ISBN- 978-1-964081-19-9 paperback
ISBN: 978-1-964081-20-5 eBook

Library of Congress Case Number 1-14524733411

Published by: HigherLife Development Services, Inc.
PO Box 623307
Oviedo, FL 32762
(407) 563-4806
www.ahigherlife.com

Printed in the United States of America
10 9 8 7 6 5 4 3 2 1

DEDICATION

This book is dedicated to my sons.
You are my greatest gifts!

ACKNOWLEDGEMENTS

Thank you to my boys for teaching me new things every day and for allowing me to share some of your stories with the world.

Tim, together we fought dragons and moved mountains. Thank you for being my safe place-through it all and for always believing in me.

Thank you to my parents for being the best Nana and Papa there ever was. Mom, you never stopped encouraging me to write this book, and I am so grateful.

To my closest friends, my home team, thank you for listening to me endlessly. Your wisdom and encouragement have made all the difference. Thank you for loving my boys so well.

Thank you to Dave, Marcy, and Michelle for hearing my heart and making this book a reality.

CONTENTS

A NOTE FROM the AUTHOR:

Hello, friend!

That is how I hope you feel after you've read this book–like you have a new friend. I, too, am a parent of a child with special needs. I, too, was once at the starting line of this race. It can be a scary and confusing place to be, but the fact that you picked up this book is evidence of the love you have for your child, and that's the best place to start!

You can read this book cover to cover or jump to whatever chapter and topics are relevant to your journey right now. I have been on both sides of the table as a special education teacher *and* as a parent. The crazy thing is, as a teacher, I felt confident in helping students and parents navigate their journeys, but when I sat in the parent seat, I desperately longed for a friend. I reached out to anyone I thought had wisdom, but finding others who had been where I was wasn't so easy. I know our stories won't be exactly alike, but I hope the words on these pages give you hope, and this little book feels like a friend holding your hand as you walk this path, especially on the most challenging days. Throw this book into your bag and know you have a friend cheering you and your child on all along the way!

Chapter 1:

THINGS NOTICED

I T WAS THANKSGIVING Day. The twins were asleep, taking a much-needed rest before the festivities began. They slept through our guests arriving. When two-and-a-half-year-old Buddy woke up, he was happy, giddy almost, to see so many people he loved in his house. His twin, Bird, woke up after his brother, and his reaction to our full house was much different. He wasn't giggling or even smiling. If I had let him, he would have hidden under his bed until the coast was clear and the house was quiet. As I carried him out of his bedroom, he tucked his head into my neck and held on tight. I sat him down, quietly letting him know who was at our house, reminding him that these guests loved him very much. He stood in the same spot, never making a sound, just staring, and plugging his ears. I smiled at him sweetly and then turned and smiled at whoever was looking at us. He was quiet and extra shy, wanting me to hold him constantly. I tried to reassure him and offered to go back to his room with him, but all he wanted to do was hide.

The day went on; we ate the turkey. Bird became more comfortable and even played outside in the backyard. Over the following couple of days, however, some of our family members started making comments.

"I think something is wrong with Bird..."

"Are you sure Bird was okay on Thursday?"

"Do you think something is wrong with his hearing?"

There were other comments, but I tried to drown them out. What did they mean that *something was wrong*? My sweet boy just got overwhelmed. He didn't like all the noise. I would have acted that way, too, if I'd woken up to all those people at my house. Sure, Bird hadn't started talking yet; he just used some unclear babble. His brother tended to talk for him. They had a language only understood by the two of them. I thought it was a cute twin thing.

But as the days went on, the fact that my mother and mother-in-law expressed concerns, people who love my son and would never want something to be wrong with him, I felt I needed to look into it. The signs weren't big and flashy, but to those who knew him best, they could tell something wasn't right. I started to notice things too but chalked it up to "that's just Bird." He was easily overstimulated in crowds or when around loud noise. I noticed how he worked hard to cope in those situations. Aware that I tend to underreact, I decided it was time for a professional opinion. The results would either prove them all wrong or help me see what I'd been missing right in front of me.

I talked with the speech therapist/pathologist that I worked with at the time. I had gone to her many times in the past year for advice. I told her some of the concerns family members had shared with me. She suggested that I get in touch with our local Early Steps program. She said they would gather information from me over the phone and set up a date and time for us to come in for evaluations. It felt good to know that, at the very least, we had a next step... to reach out and make an appointment. It was overwhelming to live in the space of "what do we do?" without any direction.

THINGS YOU CAN EXPECT

Sometimes, even if you're the parent or caregiver, others may notice things that seem "off" in your child before you do. At this stage, you can expect to get asked a lot of questions and feel a variety of emotions. You might feel defensive or protective of your child. You might feel embarrassed that you didn't notice these things sooner. Maybe you feel shocked, sad, confused, or afraid. And then there's denial—the "bliss" of refusing to believe that your child's quirks are anything other than sweet little pieces of their personality.

> It felt good to know that, at the very least, we had a next step

Whatever you are feeling, there is no right or wrong emotion. Allow yourself to feel your feelings as they come. You are at the starting line of this journey with your child. The journey may be long, with winding roads, but that doesn't mean there won't be wins and celebrations along the way. There will be!

Quick Tips

- You don't have to have all of the answers right away. This is a journey that needs to be taken one step at a time.

- Get a notebook or journal. Write down anything and everything you observe about your child. This is also a good place to write down questions you have for the pediatrician, psychologist, and other members of the intervention team.

- Find a good support system. Your support system can be made up of family and friends, but if you don't have anyone who can be that for you, you can find many online support groups through social media.

- If your child is three years old or younger, start researching what your state and county have to offer for early intervention and evaluations. A simple search on the internet can lead you to the right place.

NOTES/TAKEAWAYS

_____

_____

_____

_____

_____

_____

_____

_____

_____

_____

_____

_____

Chapter 2:

EVALUATIONS, BUT YOU KNOW YOUR CHILD BEST

GOT IN TOUCH with Early Steps at the beginning of December. We couldn't get an appointment for evaluations until mid-January. Over the phone, a registered nurse asked me tons of yes-or-no questions. Very few questions could be answered with a simple yes or no, which was eye-opening. There were a few I could answer simply: Can he put on a shirt by himself? Yes. Does he have any known allergies? No.

But the majority of the questions I wanted to explain. Does he enjoy being with friends and family? Yes, he loves his Nana and Papa very much and loves playing with his brother. However, he seems to get overwhelmed when we are together with a large group, especially in a tight space.

There was so much more I needed to say, but they required a yes or no and didn't want to hear my explanations. As soon as I started to explain an answer, they would answer for me, usually an answer I felt reflected negatively on my little boy. I felt like I was on trial, and with every "wrong" answer, the jury was giving my boy a life sentence, and it was all my fault.

There was so much more I needed to say

Being a mother means absorbing much of our children's experiences, whether or not it's our responsibility. The weight of "mom guilt" is undeniable. Answering questions without room for elaboration felt like presenting an incomplete picture of my boy. And the labels they might assign felt excessively permanent.

By the time they got to the part where I was able to explain my concerns, I felt like they had already diagnosed him. I simply answered, "I'm concerned with his speech and language; his only real word is Momma. He plugs his ears when there are loud noises and has a hard time in large crowds." I had no idea what was happening on the other end of the line. All I could do was wait until our appointment, which was set for after the holidays.

The waiting was hard and weighed heavy on both my husband and me. After having the phone conversation with the nurse, I felt like there was so much I still wanted to say and questions I wanted to ask. I like to clarify for my own understanding and peace of mind, but I wasn't able to do that on this call. Waiting for that appointment left all those things lingering on my mind.

We finally arrived at our appointment and met with the RN I'd spoken with on the phone. I was ready to find out what could be going on with my boy so I could start helping him. As hard as waiting had been, it gave me time to pause and process everything I'd seen and been through up to that point. Finally, we could start moving forward. The RN was much warmer in person. In this interaction, I felt like she was on our team.

Both boys were being evaluated that day, one at a time. Buddy went first—then it was Bird's turn. The room was small and bright: white tile, white walls, and fluorescent lighting. I sat in a chair behind Bird while he sat in a smaller chair at a table. The licensed psychologist sat in front of him on the other side of the table, and a speech pathologist and the RN sat to his right.

Bird, only two-and-a-half at that time, didn't want to stay seated in the little chair. He wanted to sit on my lap, but every time I brought him up and pulled him close, the psychologist sighed and asked me to help him refocus.

They set a stacker in front of him and removed all the rings. Bird was to place the rings back on the stacker. I silently cheered inside because we had a Mickey Mouse stacker at home that he loved to play with. Not only would he stack the rings that came with it, but he would also stack other ring-shaped items such as tape or the dog's toy. Surely that meant nothing was "wrong" with my boy, right?

Bird didn't perform. He just looked at me with sad eyes and started to come over to me. Trying to follow the psychologist's orders, I redirected him back to his seat at the table. He laid his head down on the white tile. Needless to say, he wouldn't make a stack out of the blocks when asked, even though he stacked many different types of blocks (wooden, foam, ones with letters, ones with numbers, etc.) at home all the time. He even thought it was hilarious to make a tower of blocks with his brother and then knock them over. The boys would laugh and laugh at that. How could they adequately diagnose him, if he needed one at all, if they couldn't see what he could *really* do?

The psychologist asked, "Bird, can you draw a line without making any sound?" Bird drew a line but included a "zoom" as he drew it. He didn't receive points for doing the task because he made a sound. We were presented with a score sheet at the end of the evaluations. Scores between 85-115 were considered "within normal limits." Bird's highest score of 86 was in the area of Adaptive (self-care and personal responsibility). His lowest was a 55 in Communication (receptive and expressive). A big asterisk on the scoring sheet said, "*Note: Test results of young children should be interpreted cautiously."

The boys would laugh and laugh at that.

It was written that he was able to do a lot of things, such as feeding himself, scribbling with a crayon, taking off his shoes, jumping, showing affection toward people he knows, greeting people appropriately, moving independently, playing peek-a-boo, matching shapes, looking for a missing object (but was unable to find it on his own), using gestures and pointing to make requests, and waving bye-bye.

The areas of concern were all sensory: following adult-given directions and responding to his name with eye contact. I was sick at the sight of the scores and their explanations. Shocked is probably more accurate. The scores and their explanations didn't seem to align. The scores warranted intervention, but the explanations seemed to come from a mind already made up, with or without data on the part of the psychologist. I was frustrated; I felt unheard and that my boy wasn't truly seen for who he was.

Looking back and rereading the scoring sheets, it doesn't seem like much, but that day, it appeared to me that the psychologist had already made up her mind about Bird the minute (or maybe even before) she met him. She encouraged me to fill out an M-Chat[1], a modified checklist for Autism in Toddlers ages 16-48 months of age. My husband and I filled it out right there in the tiny evaluation

---

1   The primary goal of the M-Chat is to maximize sensitivity, meaning to detect as many cases of Autism Spectrum Disorder (ASD) as possible. Therefore, there is a high false-positive rate, meaning not all children who score "at risk" will be diagnosed with ASD.

room. He only had three of the 23 indicators for autism.[2]

The psychologist suggested that Bird have a separate psychological evaluation to rule out ASD. He showed "red flags" for autism because "he failed the M-Chat, even though he fell at the lowest end of "moderate risk."

"What?" I asked. "He only has three of the indicators."

Buddy also missed some of the indicators, but they didn't even want to discuss that. They waved their hands and said he was fine and would receive speech therapy. I have a bachelor's degree in Exceptional Student Education from the University of Central Florida and was teaching ESE in the public school system. I wasn't claiming to be an expert, but I had my educated doubts. I would do what I was told to do, but not without questions.

The psychologist looked right at me and said, "You need to get over yourself and the fact that you teach special education and think you can fix him. He has an IQ of 66 and may never talk. Just get used to the fact that you may have a son

---

2   Scoring: 0-2 is low risk, 3-7 is moderate risk, and 8-20 is considered high risk.

who drools in the corner all his life." My husband had to hold me down. He actually had to place his arms on my legs to keep me in my seat. I wanted to claw that woman's eyes out. Not because my son might have autism but because of the manner in which she told me so. One of the last things I remember the psychologist saying to us is, "One positive about being autistic is that you get to ride the rides first at Disney. You get to skip the lines." She laughed.

I would do what I was told to do, but not without questions.

I opened my mouth to speak, but no words came out, only silent tears. Both boys would receive speech therapy twice a week in our home, and after having an occupational therapy (OT) evaluation, Bird would receive occupational therapy in our home as well. We were told not to have additional testing until we began those interventions.

As we made our way out of the room, I felt like my feet were dragging, but my mind was racing. Beth, the RN, walked us out to the waiting room. I looked at her, my face streaked with tears and asked her if she agreed with what was said during and after the evaluation. She looked at me with compassion in her eyes. She told me how many families come to get answers and don't feel satisfied with only early intervention. They want something more, a concrete diagnosis. ASD diagnoses are on the rise, and that is often what people are told, just as we were that day. She encouraged us to start the speech and OT interventions soon and see if these "red flags" remain or go away. We didn't have a definite diagnosis yet.

What we *did* have were more questions, confusion, and feelings of being dismissed and disregarded—more like numbers passing through a door than real people with real lives who needed a genuine listening ear and skillset to *see* our son as an individual, not lectures about "just get over yourself." Many doctors pass loads of kids through their diagnostic doors, and they are often burned out or ill-equipped. They are used to working with parents who *want* some type of diagnosis. They want answers and the support and benefits that a diagnosis offers. While I understand that this is the everyday experience of medical professionals, each new child deserves the time to be seen and parents heard. Parents who don't have a background in child development are at the mercy of these doctors.

This is not everyone's experience, but it was ours. Some families will experience a listening ear and genuine concern, and others will experience something like we did. The most important thing to remember is that you are your child's best advocate. You know your child better than anyone. It can be hard to hear difficult news or less than satisfactory solutions. You are allowed to take time after your appointment to process what you were told and make your own decisions. I'll share some tips below to help you navigate the after-evaluation experience.

> They want answers and the support and benefits that a diagnosis offers.

THINGS YOU CAN EXPECT

Don't be discouraged if you can't get an appointment right away. Sometimes, appointments are booked weeks or even months out. Your child might have already started school, either because you got a diagnosis later or because you couldn't be seen sooner.

In the days leading up to your appointment, a case manager (in our case, a registered nurse) will call and do a phone interview. During this interview, you will answer questions about your child's development and what you have observed in your child up to that point. This interview is used as a pre-screener for early intervention. Use this as an opportunity to ask questions about the evaluation and the next steps for your child. Take lots of notes and document, document, document. This can look like taking a notebook to doctor appointments and writing things down in it to journaling your thoughts and observations after the appointment. This will help you remember more of the details you need when advocating for your child. So much information is thrown at you; it's important to take time to process and decide what you agree or disagree with. Your notes will help with that. It's also important to document because it forces others to take you more seriously. Documentation equals evidence.

Take lots of notes and document, document, document.

A team of professionals will evaluate your child on the day of your appointment. A physical therapist will evaluate your child's gross motor skills. An occupational therapist will evaluate fine motor skills, as well as any sensory needs they may have. A speech therapist and/or language pathologist will evaluate your child's communication and language skills. The head of this team will be a developmental psychologist. Remember–*you* are also part of this team. You should be present during the evaluation. Your observations and concerns are most important. It's also comforting for your child to have you present.

We went through many different types of testing. Sometimes, I sat next to him, sometimes I was in a chair across the room, and sometimes I peeked in from where I couldn't be seen.

If you are not able to be next to your child during this process, talk to them ahead of time to let them know what to expect. If they are so young they won't understand, you can assure them in the moment that you will not leave them.

> I felt unheard and that my boy
> wasn't truly seen for who he was.

There is never a situation where it's better for your child to be uncomfortable or anxious. In those cases, I always question the validity of the results.

Quick Tips

- Take your notebook or journal with you. It will help you remember questions you might have. It is also a good idea to record your own observations and compare them with the final report.

- It can be intimidating to walk into a room with a large team of professionals. Take a trusted friend or family member with you so that they can be your second set of ears.

- Remember, you are the number one person on your child's team. Your input is important. Speak up, redirect, or encourage your child when needed.

NOTES/TAKEAWAYS

_____

_____

_____

_____

_____

_____

_____

_____

_____

_____

_____

Chapter 3:

EARLY INTERVENTION

BEFORE THE IN-HOME interventions could start, both boys were sent to have their hearing and vision checked. We had made an appointment before we met with Early Steps at the Children's Hospital in the city. Quickly into the testing, we were told that the boys were "too immature" to get accurate results. We had to make an appointment elsewhere to get the testing completed. This time, we went to the Audiology Center at a local public elementary school. Both the boys' vision and hearing were fine.

About three weeks later, we met with an occupational therapist named Brenda. She came to our house to complete a service evaluation of Bird. The results were that Bird had a definite sensory processing dysfunction—two standards below the mean. Brenda would be coming to our house for an hour each week to work with Bird on goals she created to help him develop sensory processing skills and strategies. This was in addition to the weekly speech therapy in our home.

Brenda came after breakfast time. Buddy was always so excited to see her. She made him feel like she was there to see him, too. Bird, on the other hand, was compliant but was worn out when she left. Her activities were work for him. Each session was filled with different activities, from writing with tiny pieces of chalk to putting his hands in shaving cream. He would crawl through a big tube and roll over a yoga ball. He would make noises with all different types of instruments. He would balance and jump. He would make decisions.

One of the lessons Brenda taught me was that I have to give the boys choices and let them (sometimes make them) decide. This not only brought them self-awareness but also helped with their speech and language too. Brenda didn't try to coddle Bird or make him feel comfortable. She never sugar-coated the information she gave me. She pushed until I thought both Bird and I might break, but we never did. Instead of breaking, we got stronger. Bird grew to tolerate sounds and activities he'd melted down over in the past. He knew what he wanted and became motivated to let us know. He was using the strategies he was learning and becoming self-aware but still couldn't verbally let us know with his words.

One night at dinner, we were all at the table. Bird was trying to tell us something in his usual babble. My husband and I tried so hard to figure out what he was saying, trying to guess or pretend we knew. He got up from the table, looked back at us, and began to sob. How frustrating it must have been for him not to be understood. This was his first breakdown and also the first time we knew for sure that he realized we couldn't understand what it was he was trying to say. This was a sign of self-awareness, for sure! But it also broke our hearts. It was also crystal clear to me that we needed to take action to help him. He didn't just need time. He needed interventions, especially in speech and language. Having speech therapy only once a week just wasn't enough. He needed more.

Early intervention is just that… the starting point of help, a kind of in-action evaluation that will let you know what you may need more or less of. In our early intervention experience, we saw the results of the work Bird was putting in during each session. After just a few sessions with the occupational therapist, Bird was becoming more independent. He wanted to do more things on his own and his confidence grew. He came such a long way in just the first few months. It's as if his thoughts slowed down, and he was able to stop, listen, and follow directions. Of course, frustration still occurred from time to time, but the meltdowns decreased as his language skills improved. The moments of frustration, sadness, and challenge, all of that helped us to understand what we needed to ask for and know how to advocate for our kiddo—like asking for more speech therapy.

> He came such a long way in
> just the first few months.

THINGS YOU CAN EXPECT

There are different ways to get early interventions into your child's life. You can be referred to a therapy practice that will schedule you to come into their office and have sessions there. There is also the option of in-home care. Until the age of three, in-home care is available and publicly funded in Florida. Call your state's Early Intervention program to see what they offer in your area. With in-home care, a therapist will come to your home and work with your child in their own environment. If your child goes to daycare while you work, therapists can also provide services there.

There are different types of services and therapists. Your child may need just one or multiple services. Occupational therapy (OT) helps people of all ages with issues that affect their everyday lives. This type of therapy focuses on motor, social, sensory, play, and cognitive skills. Physical therapy (PT) focuses on gross motor and mobility skills. Speech-language pathologists treat speech disorders and delays. This type of therapy focuses on communication, speech, language, cognition, emergent literacy, and/or feeding and swallowing.

To make these therapies most effective, parents are asked to participate in between sessions. For us, that meant having Bird make decisions in the form of "this or that," as well as teaching him to sign things such as "more," "open," "help me," "please," and "all done." Brenda taught us that if Bird couldn't use a verbal word, he had to sign what he needed. His success with her partly relied on our consistency when she wasn't with us.

Quick Tips

- You will need to decide what setting is best for your child and your family. You can choose between seeing your therapist in their office or at home. You can even schedule your child's sessions in their daycare center during the day.

- While some therapy looks like play, it is work for your child. Make sure they are well rested and not hungry going into their sessions. Provide some form of downtime after their session so they can regroup, and you can, too.

- Find a therapist who makes you and your child feel comfortable. Request a change if the therapist assigned to you isn't a good fit. There are usually multiple therapists within each company. It can feel uncomfortable to ask, but it's in your child's best interest to have a good-fit therapist.

NOTES/TAKEAWAYS

_____

_____

_____

_____

_____

_____

_____

_____

_____

_____

_____

_____

Chapter 4:

ALL GOOD THINGS MUST COME to an END: TRANSITIONS

B RENDA, OUR OT, suggested we look into starting the boys in preschool because they were almost three years old, and their covered services would soon change. I thought, *NO WAY! My babies aren't ready for that. I* wasn't ready for that. As a compromise, I decided to take the boys to speech therapy at the local elementary school by our house. I figured this would give them some exposure to a school setting without committing to the entire preschool program.

They went twice a week. After we signed them in, the speech therapist would come to take us to her room, where she held sessions. She insisted that the boys sit up at the table and focus. There were tons of toys on the shelves in the room, but these were not for playing with, and she refused to allow them to sit on the floor. It just wasn't working. Expecting two-year-olds to sit in a room of toys they couldn't touch and in hard seats at a hard table and learn to speak wasn't realistic or supportive. The boys weren't benefiting, and it felt like we were wasting precious time.

I knew it was time to look for another option. With the boys getting closer to three years old, we were about to lose our in-home services.

Maybe Brenda was right... maybe it was time to consider preschool. But how would I get them ready for such a change? How would I get *myself* ready for such a change? It was scary to think about starting over with new therapists in a new setting.

> But how would I get them ready for such a change? How would I get *myself* ready for such a change?

Fortunately, none of us have to recreate the wheel on getting our kids from home to preschool or other out-of-the-house programs. It's been done, and I will walk you through how we did it.

THINGS YOU CAN EXPECT

Once a child reaches the age of three, in-home therapy is no longer covered, but you still have options! You can pay for these services in your home or transition to a different setting. Change and transitioning can be tough, but not as tough as continuing in a setting that isn't working. Not all therapists or therapy settings are right for your child. Be willing to be courageous to speak up when something isn't working.

Quick Tips

- Harness your courage to speak up when you realize something isn't working well.

- You may have to try a variety of therapists and settings before finding the right fit.

- You have options. You can pay for a therapist to come to your home or the school or daycare your child attends. You can take your child to the local school or a therapy office for their sessions.

- Every new school year is a transition when you have a child with any type of diagnosis (learning or health). You must advocate for your child at the beginning of every new school year. Consider writing a note/email to the teacher(s) before the school year begins, scheduling a conference with the teacher(s) at the beginning of the school year, and updating your child's learning plan/504/IEP.

NOTES/TAKEAWAYS

Chapter 5:

PRE-SCHOOL and CONTINUING INTERVENTIONS

B RENDA TOLD ME about Easterseals, a child
development center about thirty minutes
from our home, where she was one of the
occupational therapists and where they could get
speech therapy as well. After the holidays, I went
to check out the facility. Although it was small, it
was much bigger than the safety of our home. I was
nervous, but I knew I had to give it a try. The boys
were now three-and-a-half, and Bird still wasn't
talking with words we could understand. While
Bird was beginning to use some words, Buddy was
talking in full sentences (although it was still hard
to understand him sometimes). He talked so much
more than Bird and probably often *for* Bird.

The boys started going three days a week from

8:00 a.m. until noon. There were four teachers in the boys' classroom alone. I wrote each teacher a note to read on the first day of class. I was sending my little boys off for the first time, and I wanted their teachers to know a little about them.

They sang, danced, and worked in large and small groups to learn not only the academics of letters and sounds but also social skills that included a lot of communication. Their teachers sent them home each day with a note telling me what they were working on. I could see they were thriving. They had teachers who understood them and appropriately challenged them.

Brenda taught me that the boys needed choices, and sometimes those choices needed to be challenging and not necessarily something they'd like. I saw this same theory being applied in their classroom. I felt safe having the boys there, not only because of the way the classroom was set up but because Easterseals believes that the "First Five Count."[3] They believe "the first five years of life lay the foundation for a child's long-term well-being and overall success." They help children

---

3 Make the first five count for child development. Easterseals. (n.d.). https://www.easterseals.com/mtffc/.

"start kindergarten with the right skills to succeed along with their peers." This is exactly what we wanted for our kids and what they needed.

Looking back, sending both boys to preschool was the right choice! After this experience, I think preschool is so important for all children, not just those with developmental delays or any other type of disability. I think families should observe any place where they are going to send their child. Meet the teachers, see other students in action, and ask questions. I went once on my own and once with the boys. The child needs to observe before going too, allowing them to know what to expect on their first day.

THINGS YOU CAN EXPECT

Sending your child to school can be a very scary decision. Full- and part-time schedules are offered in many pre-schools. Again, you get to decide this because you know your child best. Part-time can be the number of days or hours your child attends.

Looking back, sending both boys to preschool was the right choice!

If your child is there during lunchtime, you will need to decide what to send them for lunch. Many places offer lunch, but if your child has sensory needs, packing lunch or even extra snacks might be a good idea. I packed the boys' lunch but encouraged their teachers to let them try whatever the prepared lunch was for the day. Remember, giving choices is so powerful.

Quick Tips

- Tour the school you are interested in. First, go without your child so that you can ask any questions and scope it out without distractions. Then, take a second tour, this time with your child in tow, so they know what to expect.

- Write a letter to your child's teacher so they can refer back to it throughout those first weeks. This will help the teacher get to know your child quicker than through observation alone and will also put your mind at ease.

- If naptime is part of the preschool routine, pack a comfort item for your child to have during this time. It can be a comfortable blanket, a small pillow, or even a stuffed animal.

NOTES/TAKEAWAYS

Chapter 6:

KINDERGARTEN and BEYOND: YOU ARE YOUR CHILD'S ADVOCATE

I F SENDING THE boys to preschool was a big step, kindergarten felt like an even bigger leap. They were small, very small, fish in a big pond. The class size was bigger, and they would be there all day, all week. It seemed like a lot, but it was the next step we had to take. At this time, home-schooling or private schools were not an option for us. So, off to public school they went. I must also mention that I was a teacher at their public school at the time. This made drop-off easier in some ways but made other things more difficult.

It was important for us to meet with the teacher and let her know about our sensory boy and what our path had been up to that point. We were lucky to get a teacher who was the best of the best, in my opinion. She listened and asked questions as they came up throughout the year. I am forever grateful she allowed me to be part of some big decisions. The structure and predictability of her classroom made for a positive experience because it felt safe for both me and my boys.

Unfortunately, in public school, you don't get to deal solely with the classroom teacher. You have special area teachers who teach physical education, music, and art and also see students each week. This may not be the case for you, but this is where the trouble lies for my sensory boy. Physical education is hot, especially in Florida, where we live, and many of the activities include yelling and cheering, which can be extra loud to a child with sensory issues.

> I am forever grateful she allowed me to be part of some big decisions.

Another issue is that transitions between subjects can breed anxiousness. This makes my boy feel like he needs to use the restroom. So even if he goes right before he leaves class, he will most likely have to go again when he gets to the new location. I understand that students only have limited time in these special area classes, but this bathroom issue became much bigger than necessary. We were asked to bring in a doctor's note so he could use the bathroom when he needed to. Our pediatrician happily provided a note, and into his file it went. Problem solved, right?! Nope. If my son asked to use the bathroom while in PE, he could go but had to run a lap. The music teacher went as far as to say he could go when needed, but it would affect his grade. Something as simple as bathroom breaks was crushing my son's school spirit. He was always anxious on the days he had those classes. It shouldn't have been a battle, but it was. Watching my young son lack the support and understanding of an informed educational team was frustrating and hurtful. It felt like a power struggle instead of secure, caring adults supporting a child with unique needs by letting him use the restroom. I knew the boys and I couldn't stay in an educational culture like that. When advocacy is ineffective, and a school doesn't want to grow, it may be time to go.

THINGS YOU CAN EXPECT

I'm not sure what difficulties your child might face when they enter grade school for the first time, but you are your child's best advocate! You want school to be a positive environment for your child, and if it isn't, schedule a meeting and don't be afraid to request that the administration or a guidance counselor be present. Working at the same school for many years before my boys attended, it was tough feeling like I was stepping on toes, or I might make someone dislike me. I had to remind myself every day what my priorities were. My kids' success had to come before my comfort zone. Change and transitions can be hard for any child, even if you get the best teachers. Meet with the teacher or teachers as close to the start of the school year as you can. Becoming an educational team will set your student up for success.

You want school to be a positive environment for your child.

Quick Tips

- Attend the Meet the Teacher night or Open House before the first day of school. This will give both you and your child a chance to learn where their class is located, meet the teacher, and, hopefully, see where they will sit on the first day of school. Knowing what to expect can help put everyone a little more at ease.

- Set up a conference with your child's teacher as close to the start of school as possible. The teacher needs to know the details that will help your student succeed.

- Get to know all of the people who will be working with your child. That includes their classroom teacher, special area teachers, special education teachers, and therapists they will see in the school setting. It is important to create a strong educational team with open communication. It is easier to do this when you know the people on your team.

- YOU are your child's BEST advocate. You know all the important details. Trust your instincts when making decisions for them; when something isn't right, harness your courage and speak up.

NOTES/TAKEAWAYS

_____

_____

_____

_____

_____

_____

_____

_____

_____

_____

_____

Chapter 7

ACCOMMODATIONS in the CLASSROOM

MOST STUDENTS WITH special needs will need accommodations in their classroom setting. Accommodations are changes to how a student receives information without changing what is being taught or the learning goal. Accommodations change *how* a student learns, not what they learn.

There are different types of accommodations.

Presentation accommodations benefit those who have difficulty taking in information. They may have visual impairments or trouble processing their thoughts while doing another task, such as writing an essay or taking notes. Presentation accommodations address how the information is presented. Some examples of this type of accommodation are allowing the student to take pictures of the notes instead of writing them down, giving a written list of instructions instead of just listening to them given out loud, or having test questions read aloud. This can also include having a note-taker take notes for the child, enlarged print size, color contrast settings on the computer, highlighting, or repeated instructions.

Accommodations change how a student learns, not what they learn.

Response accommodations help students show what they know in a variety of possible ways. Students who have visual perception disabilities or attention span difficulties benefit from these accommodations. Response accommodations deal with how the student completes an assignment. An example of this type of accommodation is allowing a student to record or type their answers on an assignment or test instead of having to handwrite them out. You can also have dictation response to a scribe, speech-to-text technology, pencil grips and other handwriting support, and additional wait time for a student response.

Setting accommodations help students who are easily distracted or struggle to focus. This can be the seating location, where the student is, and where tasks and activities take place. This can refer to in-class seating arrangements, small group instruction, small group or one-on-one testing, and location during tests to best eliminate distractions. This can also include lighting or other sensory accommodations, noise-reducing headphones, increased opportunity for movement, and consistent and predictable routines.

Scheduling accommodations involve how a student's time and schedule are organized. For example, a student may be allowed extra time on graded assignments and testing, or breaks, especially if they have attention span and focusing difficulties.

Accommodations are individualized and based on the needs of the individual student. It's important to know that accommodations need to be used in the student's natural environment and daily classroom routine and not only on district or state testing.

Modifications are different from accommodations. Modifications actually change *what* the student is learning. These can include alternate assignments, projects, test questions, and even what standards and benchmarks are taught.

Modifications are different
from accommodations.

The accommodation we needed and most fought for was for one-on-one testing. This falls under the category of Flexible Setting. I understand this takes time and personnel–it's often more about funding and staffing because it takes more than the classroom teacher to accomplish this. As a result, I was told each year that the school didn't have the resources, and each year I pushed back. Not because I was a pain or wanted my way, but because my son needed this accommodation in order to show what he really knew when being assessed. With his diagnosis, noises were his ultimate distraction. He could hear a fly buzzing on the other side of the classroom or a pencil sharpener down the hall and lose focus. It's hard not to take these fights personally, but when it's your baby, it is personal.

We eventually received this accommodation, but not without a fight. Each year at the IEP meeting, I had to advocate for him to receive it. It made such a difference in my son demonstrating what he actually knew on a test without all the distractions.

THINGS YOU CAN EXPECT

In order to put new accommodations or modifications in place, you will need to meet with the classroom team and possibly other specialists who make up the educational team. Come prepared with your observations and why your student needs these changes to be successful. You are a vital part of this team!

Quick Tips

- While accommodations and modifications aren't served buffet style, there are many different ways to help your student succeed in the classroom.

- You may think your student needs a specific accommodation or modification, but the school team disagrees. Be prepared to explain your reasons and know that it's okay to push back rather than just accept no for an answer.

- Needs change over time. It's okay to try something until it no longer works and then try something different.

NOTES/TAKEAWAYS

_____

_____

_____

_____

_____

_____

_____

_____

_____

_____

_____

_____

Chapter 8

IEP: GOALS and MEETINGS

O NCE YOUR CHILD reaches the age of three, they will need an Individualized Educational Plan (IEP). This is a legal document that maps out the instruction, support, and services your child will receive. An educational team will work together to create this. You, the caregiver, are an integral part of this team! The team is also made up of a general education teacher and a special education teacher who work with your student. Others who may make up this team include therapists that your child works with (occupational, speech and language, and/or physical), as well as a professional who will help you make sense of it all. This may be a school guidance counselor, psychologist, or staffing specialist.

Going into these meetings can be intimidating—even for a parent who is also a special education teacher. In the morning, I would be part of meetings for my own classroom students and was treated as if I were the wisest person in the room. The others would look to me for answers, and they would value my opinions. Then the afternoon would come, and I'd be sitting on the other side of the table. This time, I was in the spot of the caregiver and not the educator. Man, how the winds shifted quickly. I was no longer the one with knowledge and wisdom in the eyes of this team. Disclaimer: I am not saying this will be the case for you or the way every team runs. This is just my experience, friend, and I want to be open with you. There can appear to be a hierarchy on these teams. Regardless of where you feel you've been placed in the hierarchy; you *are* the most knowledgeable of your own child in that room. You are the decision-maker in this meeting. *YOU* are inviting this team into the care and support of your child with their unique skillset and training. No matter how the dynamic of the room feels, this is the reality.

You, the caregiver, are an integral part of this team!

As the parent in these IEP meetings, I had to harness my courage again and again. One of the best ways I know how to do that is by being prepared. I would spend the weeks leading up to the meeting keeping a journal of sorts in a notebook that I brought along with me. I wrote down things I saw, both the strengths and growth, as well as the struggles my sensory boy was experiencing. This helped me give my input on the current level of performance and helped to justify the need for specific goals and accommodations that would be on the updated IEP. There is something about documenting things in writing that makes your words even more powerful than if you were to only speak to them.

I had to harness my courage
again and again.

The team, and that includes you, will come up with goals and objectives that will be on the IEP. Goals will focus on the skills that need support. Goals must be measurable. That means that the student's progress can be observed. To be measurable, the goal must state the area of the need.

This could be the subject or class. The goal must state the direction of the goal using words such as increase, decrease, and maintain. The goal must also include the specific level of attainment, whether that is age or grade level, or the percent of accuracy. The goal should tell who (the student), the timeframe in which the goal is to be completed, and who is responsible for measuring progress. This could be a teacher and/or therapist.

Accommodations for scheduling, setting, responding, and presentation will also be listed on the IEP.

If you're not comfortable with the IEP or feel pressured to add or remove things, you do not have to sign. You can ask for more time and request changes until you feel comfortable signing your agreement. This goes back to coming in prepared. Be prepared to say no and not sign if you're not ready.

THINGS YOU CAN EXPECT

Individualized Education Plans are updated annually. You will receive an invitation to the meeting in advance, and you can agree or disagree with the date and time. You can also attend by phone or not at all. Once you attend the meeting, the IEP presented to you is only a draft. A final copy will not be printed or submitted until all of it has been reviewed and discussed with the whole team.

Quick tips

- IEP goals are revised once a year, but you can request a review meeting at any time.

- If you do not agree with the IEP for any reason, you can write "not in agreement" next to where you will need to sign. Your signature shows that you attended the meeting.

- PLOP stands for the student's Present Level of Performance. This covers curriculum and learning, social and emotional behavior, independent functioning, health care, communication, self-determination, and the student's priority education needs.

- You are an important part of the team and your voice matters. If you want to bring a family member, friend, or advocate with you, make sure to add that to the meeting invitation sent to you in the weeks before the meeting.

NOTES/TAKEAWAYS

_____

_____

_____

_____

_____

_____

_____

_____

_____

_____

_____

_____

_____

Chapter 9:

FINAL WORDS of ENCOURAGEMENT

I GOT THE NUDGE and tapping on my heart to write this book when my sons were four years old. I was signing them into their preschool class, and a couple of professionals from the education department were there to observe. They were having a side conversation with one another about one of the students. Their conversation revolved around giving the child a label/diagnosis, lowering the bar for expected achievements, and then moving the child on. Maybe they were trying to find the best solution for that child, but from that moment on, my momma's heart bled for any and all kids who are unfairly diagnosed or diagnosed, and then the bar set for their life is lowered.

This has happened not once but twice with my

own son. If I had listened to and believed what I was told would be his future, I don't know who my son would be today. I was told he would never be able to talk and that he'd always be the kid in the corner drooling.

He's now thirteen and in the eighth grade. He talks all the time, has appropriate conversations, and asks appropriate questions. He's funny. He's smart. He can do math in his head and has an incredible memory. He definitely doesn't drool, and you won't find him in the corner. He loves people, making friends, and helping others to feel included.

Do I still have to push and fight at times for accommodations? Yes! But he is excelling in school and in life, and he has the mindset that he can be and do anything he sets his mind to. I didn't allow him to be put into a box, and I encourage you not to put your child in a box, either. Every year, there are more and more options for all students, ones with and without a diagnosis, which can give them hope for a future.

He loves people, making friends, and helping others to feel included.

Will my son's outcome look like everyone else's? Of course not. But I believe every child should have the opportunity to flourish in their best, unique way without the world around them expecting the least of them.

Writing this book was a calling put on my heart; if you've read it, it was meant for you!

Having journeyed through the pages of this book, I hope that you now feel the warmth of camaraderie and the assurance that you are not alone. As a fellow parent of a child with special needs, I stood at the starting line just like you. It's a place filled with uncertainty and fear, but the very act of picking up this book is a testament to the deep love you hold for your child—a love that serves as the best starting point.

Whether you read this book cover to cover or navigated to specific chapters relevant to your current journey, I want you to know that I've stood on both sides of the table as a special education teacher and parent. Despite my confidence in guiding students and their parents in my role as a teacher, sitting in the parent's seat left me yearning for companionship. I sought wisdom from anyone I believed could offer it, realizing that finding those who had walked a similar path wasn't as simple as I had hoped.

While our stories may not align perfectly, I trust that the words within these pages have sparked a sense of hope within you. May this little book be like a faithful friend, holding your hand as you navigate this challenging path, particularly on the toughest days. Tuck this book into your bag, knowing that you have a friend cheering you and your child on every step of the way.

NOTES/TAKEAWAYS

_____

_____

_____

_____

_____

_____

_____

_____

_____

_____

_____

_____

_____

REFERENCES

Easterseals
https://www.easterseals.com

AMA (Find a Doctor near you)
https://find-doctor.ama-assn.org/

The Arc (Find resources in your area)
https://thearc.org/find-resources/

Family Voices (Family Voices is a national family-led organization of families and friends of children and youth with special health care needs (CYSHCN) and disabilities.
https://familyvoices.org/

National Center for Learning Disabilities
https://www.ncld.org

Boys and Girls Club of America
bgca.org

Learning Disabilities Association of Florida
https://lda-florida.org/

TOGETHER WE ARE
ALL STRONGER!

CONTINUE the CONVERSATION

If you enjoyed this book, please consider sharing:

- Leave a 5-star review on Amazon or other online retailers

- Mention this book on your blog, (X)Twitter, Instagram, and Facebook page.

- Suggesting The Empowered Parent to friends and send them to the publisher's website.

- Bulk copies can be purchased through the publisher's website: https://www.higherlifepublishing.com